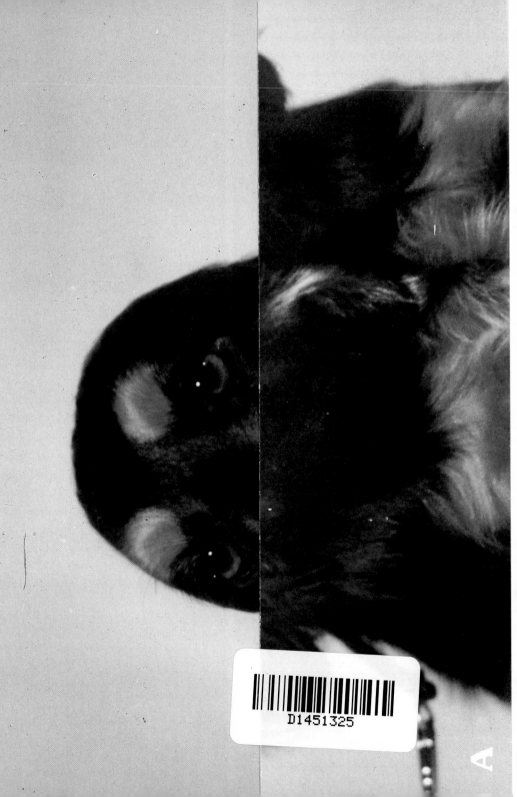

Cocker Spaniels

E·H·HART

Edited by the Staff of T.F.H. Publications

The sections titled "History of the Cocker Spaniel" and "Grooming Your Cocker Spaniel" have been written by Bart King. The rest of the book was compiled and edited by various members of the full-time staff of T.F.H. Publications, Inc. This new edition has been enhanced with full-color photographs and pull-out posters.

Distributed in the UNITED STATES by T.F.H. Publications, Inc., 211 West Sylvania Avenue, Neptune City, NJ 07753; in CANADA by H & L Pet Supplies Inc., 27 Kingston Crescent, Kitchener, Ontario N2B 2T6; Rolf C. Hagen Ltd., 3225 Sartelon Street, Montreal 382 Quebec; in ENGLAND by T.F.H. Publications Limited, 4 Kier Park, Ascot, Berkshire SL5 7DS; in AUSTRALIA AND THE SOUTH PACIFIC by T.F.H. (Australia) Pty. Ltd., Box 149, Brookvale 2100 N.S.W., Australia; in NEW ZEALAND by Ross Haines & Son, Ltd., 18 Monmouth Street, Grey Lynn, Auckland 2 New Zealand; in SINGAPORE AND MALAYSIA by MPH Distributors (S) Pte., Ltd., 601 Sims Drive, # 03/07/21, Singapore 1438; in the PHILIPPINES by Bio-Research, 5 Lippay Street, San Lorenzo Village, Makati Rizal; in SOUTH AFRICA by Multipet Pty. Ltd., 30 Turners Avenue, Durban 4001. Published by T.F.H. Publications Inc., Ltd. the British Crown Colony of Hong Kong.

Contents

Poster **A**—A member of the sporting group
of dog breeds, the Cocker Spaniel has a well-
developed nose. Photo by Ake Wintzell.

Poster **B**—A Cocker Spaniel can excel as a
show dog, a sporting dog, and an obedience
dog as well. This solid colored Cocker is
owned by Joy Yard, Howell, New Jersey.
Photo by Vince Serbin.

Poster **C**—Two magnificent Cocker Spaniels;
parti-colored black and white and a solid
colored black. Photo by Ake Wintzell.

Introduction

The proper introduction to a book like this one is a list of other good books about dogs, because no relatively small book could hope to cover comprehensively all of the specialized topics that a serious dog fancier can become involved with. Breeding, training, exhibiting, health care—they're all important topics, each one deserving a big volume of its own for proper exposition. The following books are all published by T.F.H. Publications and are recommended to you for additional information.

Dog Behavior, Why Dogs Do What They Do by Dr. Ian Dunbar (H-1016) is a thorough and enlightening exploration of all aspects of canine behavior and the relationship between man and dog. The author, a noted specialist in the field of animal behavior, discusses canine communication, social and sexual behaviors, and the physical and sensory capacities and capabilities of dogs, among other topics.

Dog Training by Lew Burke (H-962) reveals the secrets behind the methods successfully used by the author, a premier trainer of dogs for individuals, industry, and the government. Lew Burke concentrates on understanding dogs' needs in relation to the needs of their owner, and he uses dogs' psychological makeup to keep dogs happy by being obedient.

All About Dog Shows by Sam Kohl (PS-778) is a highly informative as well as entertaining introduction to dog shows. Written for the visitor to a dog show and for the beginning exhibitor, the book is illustrated with satirical pen-and-ink sketches of dogs and their exhibitor-owners.

Successful Dog Show Exhibiting by Anna Katherine Nicholas (H-993) is an excellent how-to manual for purebred dog owners who are thinking about entering the world of dog show competition. The book includes detailed explanations of dog show classes, step-by-step descriptions of the judging process (including what the judge looks for), ring behavior do's and don'ts for both dog and handler, and advantages and disadvantages of professional handlers versus showing your own dog. The author, a judge who's been part of the world of dogs for over 50 years, knows her subject well and makes it understandable for the reader.

Dog Breeding for Professionals by Dr. Herbert Richards (H-969) is a straightforward discussion of how to breed dogs of various sizes and how to care for newborn puppies. The many aspects of breeding (including

Introduction

possible problems and practical solutions) are covered in great detail. The explicit photos of canine sexual activities may offend some readers.

Dog Owner's Encyclopedia of Veterinary Medicine by Allan H. Hart, B.V.Sc. (H-934) is a comprehensive treatise on canine disease and disorders. It is written on the premise that dog owners should recognize the symptoms and understand the treatments of most diseases of dogs, so that dog owners can properly communicate with their veterinarian or give treatment to their dogs. Proper nutrition, parasite problems, and first-aid measures are also described.

• • •

In addition to the foregoing, the following individual breed books of interest to readers of this book are available at pet shops and book stores.

The Book of the Cocker Spaniel
By Joan McDonald Brearley
ISBN 0-87666-737-x
TFH H-1034

Contents: The History Of The Breed. The Cocker Spaniel In England. The Cocker Spaniel Arrives In America. The American Spaniel Club. The Cocker Spaniel As A Breed. Cocker Spaniel People And Places. Buying Your Cocker Spaniel. Grooming Your Cocker Spaniel. The Dog Show World. Showing And Judging The Cocker Spaniel. Cocker Spaniel Show Dog Statistics. Cocker Spaniels In Obedience. Cocker Spaniels In The Field. Breeding Your Cocker Spaniels. Feeding And Nutrition. The Blight Of Parasites. Your Dog, Your Veterinarian And You. Pursuing A Career In Dogs.
Hard cover, 8½ × 11"; 300 pages Hundreds of black and white photos; also contains many full-color photos.

The Cocker Spaniel Handbook
By Ernest H. Hart
ISBN 0-87666-270-X
TFH H-923

Contents: Genealogy Of The Cocker Spaniel. Early History Of The Cocker Spaniel. Inheritance In The Cocker Spaniel. Basic Breeding Techniques. Feeding. General Care. The Brood Bitch. The Stud Dog. Your Cocker Puppy. Fundamental Training For The Cocker Spaniel. Training For The Show Ring. Training The Cocker Spaniel For The Field. Official Standard Of The Cocker Spaniel.
Hard cover, 5½ × 8", 256 pages 174 black and white photos, 19 line illustrations

The Cocker Spaniel has, for many years, been in the list of the top ten most popular dog breeds. He is medium-sized and very adaptable, and he can be trained to display a wide range of talents. All in all, the Cocker Spaniel is a wonderful companion both in the home and outdoors. Drawing by Elinor Warren.

History of the Cocker Spaniel

No one knows the beginnings of the close association between humans and dogs, but the relationship must have extended thousands of years prior to our earliest records. The most ancient of the sculptures and bas-reliefs, more frequently than not, show a dog in the scene. From that beginning the canine family has developed and produced so many true-to-type families that the American Kennel Club now recognizes well over 100 separate breeds. There are also several breeds not so recognized by that club.

Many of the dog breeds of today are "manufactured" breeds. Man, visualizing in his mind's eye his ideal dog to suit a given purpose, proceeded to interbreed two or more distinct breeds or types until in the progeny he found a pair that fit his picture. As succeeding progeny more closely approached the end sought, the lesser specimens were culled out and the better ones bred until finally the planned breed, with type firmly fixed, resulted. Within an already established breed, if a breeder wanted to increase the size of his dogs, for instance, he would select and breed only the larger specimens.

The Spaniel Family

Spaniels comprise a very old dog family. No one knows for sure when or where they originated. Spaniels are mentioned in writings of the fourteenth century, and that's far enough back for this writer. They are commonly supposed to have been a Spanish family, although several early spaniels were found in Switzerland and France. The earliest drawings available make them look more like a "ratty" setter than a spaniel; taller and rangier, with a full-length tail carrying something of a flag and with comparatively short ears.

The Brittany is just one of several members of the Spaniel family, of which the Cocker Spaniel is a prominent member. Drawing by Ed Stevenson.

History of the Cocker Spaniel

As civilization progressed and people became intrigued with the idea of producing "man made" breeds, Spaniels were taken across Europe and into the hands of breeders in England; most of the separation of the general Spaniel family into many separate and distinct breeds originated there. Today there are such distinct Spaniel breeds as the American Water, Brittany, Clumber, Cocker, English Cocker, English Springer, Field, Irish Water, Sussex, and Welsh Springer.

In the early days of attaching subtitles to the Spaniels, it was common practice to have Cockers, Springers, etc., come out of a single litter, the only difference being size. Then as dog shows came into being and refinements were bred into the various strains, the prefixes stuck, and breed by breed the individual Spaniels came be be separated from the whole family. It was not until 1883 that Cockers were given their own classification in the shows, and ten years later before they were recognized as a distinct breed in the English stud book.

Cockers in the United States

It was sometime in the 1880's that the first Cockers came to the United States, and the famous Obo dogs set the pattern for what is now known in the United States as the Cocker Spaniel. It should be noted here that this version of the breed is called the American Cocker Spaniel by British dog fanciers. (It also should be noted that a breed known as the Cocker Spaniel in Great Britain is called the English Cocker Spaniel by Americans.)

Years ago, when Americans were importing many Cockers from England, both American and English Cockers were entered indiscriminately in the dog shows as Cocker Spaniels. A breeder could take his choice and enter one dog from a litter as an English Cocker and another from the same litter as an American Cocker. Now they are separate and distinct breeds, and interbreeding is forbidden.

It was in 1920 that Red Brucie arrived on the scene, and the Cocker started his complete change in appearance. He came along at just the right time, and, being a very prepotent dog, really gave Cockers a "new look": up on leg, shorter in the back, with a longer neck sloping into trim, tight shoulders. Not a champion himself, he nevertheless set an all-breed record for his time by siring thirty-eight champions.

Description of the Breed

Originally, the Cocker Spaniel was a gun dog, developed and used mainly in England on upland game; hence his designation as a "Cocking" Spaniel, later to be contracted to "Cocker." This bit of history ties in with character, because gun dogs must be of a high degree of intelligence and readily trainable, possessed of an aggressive yet steady temperament.

That, indeed, is a good description of the character of the Cocker Spaniel— happy, very bright, loyal, and understanding of his master's moods or the task of the moment. His size, physical beauty, and temperament soon attracted wide attention as the ideal family companion. As time passed, the Cocker came to be accepted for that place in the canine picture, and his use in the field became more and more infrequent. We must bear in mind in that connection that up until about 1925 Cockers were much smaller than they are today, and much longer in the back than they were high at the shoulder. So it is not to be wondered at that the early cockers, though they had the nose and the heart for field work (and loved it) would be passed by in favor of their big brothers, the Springers and the other sporting Spaniel breeds.

The well-rounded, appealing personality of the Cocker Spaniel has helped make this breed a popular family pet.

An Adaptable Gun Dog

In more recent years, with Cockers of thirty-five pounds the rule rather than the exception, and with body proportions brought into balance so that today they are about as high at the shoulder as they are long in back, there has been quite a resurgence in field trial activity. With a very serious-minded group determined to re-establish the Cocker's place among the gun dogs, considerable headway is being made in that direction. The fact remains that it is his adaptability as the family companion that has made him so popular.

Description of the Breed

Let's keep in mind, however, the fact that the Cocker is primarily a gun dog—not a lap dog, and not a toy. It is the Cocker's in-between size plus his irresistible disposition that is responsible for his popularity as the family companion. He is small enough so that he creates no domestic housing problem and can live in the home with the family without special arrangements having to be made for him. On the other, he is large enough to be rugged, well able to take weather, and definitely not a toy to be bundled up when he goes out into the cold.

A Cocker in the Family

The Cocker Spaniel is a wonderful children's dog and loves to romp with them. On the other hand, he is equally exuberant and happy tramping the woods and fields with the master of the household, busily smelling out the gamy scents his keen nose detects.

The Cocker adapts to most environments, and thousands of them spend their lives in super-heated apartments, always taken out on a leash and never enjoying the slightest freedom to follow their natural instincts. The reason that the Cocker is so adaptable is that primarily he is happy just to be close to his family, but that does not mean that family life finds him at his best or that is completely happy in it. Rather, he settles into a life of boredom which presents no challenge to his sharp mentality.

The Cocker Spaniel is an obedience trial dog par excellence, and few breeds have better records in the obedience trials. In training, either for the field or for obedience, hard-headedness is always a problem to the trainer, who has to force the training down the dog's throat in spite of his disinterest or unwillingness. Fortunately that characteristic is entirely foreign to the Cocker's nature. He takes to training with vim, enjoying every minute of it with his stub of a tail beating a mile a minute. Again, he'll break his neck to please his master and is never happier than when he can be with him with a job to do.

Housing for Your Cocker

No special housing is necessary for the Cocker Spaniel. He can live in a heated apartment or in an unheated outside kennel in sub-zero weather. But he must be acclimated gradually to one or the other with no sudden shifts. If a Cocker is kept

Description of the Breed

The Cocker Spaniel is a hardy breed and can live happily in warm or cold climates. He must, however, be allowed to adjust gradually to extremes in temperature.

out-of-doors in northern areas in the winter, he must have a small (large enough to stand up, lie down, and turn around, but no larger) kennel with several thicknesses of burlap sacking tacked across the top of the door, so that it will fall back into place after the dog has entered. There should be a goodly quantity of straw into which the dog can burrow. Also, he must have plenty of room to run and exercise. A dog living outside in the winter must not be tied up; he must be able to run to keep the blood circulating.

Standards for the Breed

A breed standard is the criterion by which the appearance (and to a certain extent, the temperament as well) of any given dog is made subject to objective measurement. Basically, the standard for any breed is a definition of the perfect dog, to which all specimens of the breed are compared.

Both the American Kennel Club and the Kennel Club of Great Britain have approved standards for the Cocker Spaniel, although it should be noted that in England the breed is known as the *American Cocker Spaniel*. The requirements as given in both standards are essentially the same, except that the British version permits a small amount of white on the chest and throat of a solid-colored dog, and is somewhat more liberal concerning maximum height by simply penalizing rather than disqualifying excessive height. It is, of course, recommended that the owner of a Cocker become thoroughly familiar with the official standard of the national club under which the dog is registered or will be shown.

The A.K.C. Standard

General Appearance: The Cocker Spaniel is the smallest member of the Sporting Group. He has a sturdy, compact body and a cleanly chiseled and refined head, with the overall dog in complete balance and of ideal size. He stands well up at the shoulder on straight forelegs with a topline sloping slightly toward strong, muscular quarters. He is a dog capable of considerable speed, combined with great endurance. Above all he must be free and merry, sound, well balanced throughout, and in action show a keen inclination to work; equable in temperament with no suggestion of timidity.

Head: To attain a well-proportioned head, which must be in balance with the rest of the dog, it embodies the following:

Skull: Rounded but not exaggerated with no tendency toward flatness; the eyebrows are clearly defined with a pronounced stop. The bony structure beneath the eyes is well chiseled with no prominence in the cheeks.

Muzzle: Broad and deep, with square, even jaws. The upper lip is full and of sufficient depth to cover the lower jaw. To be in correct balance, the distance from the stop to the tip of the nose is one half the distance from the stop up over the crown to the base of the skull.

Teeth: Strong and sound, not too small, and meet in a scissors bite.

12

Standards for the Breed

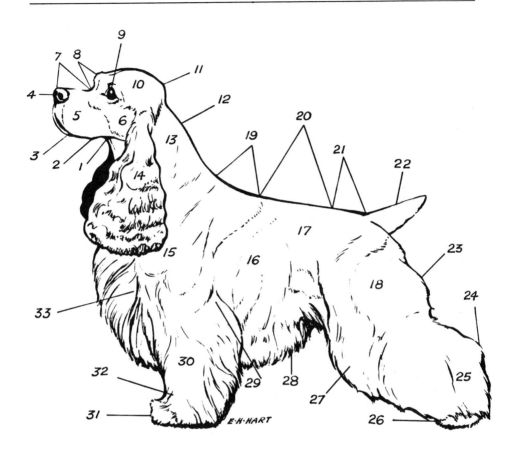

Parts of the Cocker Spaniel: 1. Throat. 2. Lip corner (flew). 3. Underjaw. 4. Nose. 5. Muzzle. 6. Cheek. 7. Foreface. 8. Stop. 9. Eye. 10. Skull. 11. Occiput. 12. Crest (of neck). 13. Neck. 14. Ear (leather). 15. Shoulder. 16. Ribs (ribbing). 17. Loin. 18. Thigh. 19. Withers. 20. Back. 21. Croup. 22. Tail (stern). 23. Feathering. 24. Hock joint. 25. Hock. 26. Feet (paws). 27. Stifle. 28. Bottom line. 29. Elbow. 30. Forearm. 31. Feet (paws). 32. Pastern. 33. Forechest.

Standards for the Breed

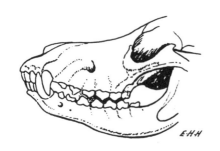

The scissors bite, the correct position for the Cocker's teeth.

Nose: Of sufficient size to balance the muzzle and foreface, with well-developed nostrils typical of a sporting dog. It is black in color in the blacks and black and tans. In other colors it may be brown, liver or black, the darker the better. The color of the nose harmonizes with the color of the eye rim.

Eyes: Eyeballs are round and full and look directly forward. The shape of the eye rims gives a slightly almond-shaped appearance; the eye is not weak or goggled. The color of the iris is dark brown and in general the darker the better. The expression is intelligent, alert, soft and appealing.

Ears: Lobular, long, of fine leather, well feathered, and placed no higher than a line to the lower part of the eye.

Neck and Shoulders: The neck is sufficiently long to allow the nose to reach the ground easily, muscular and free from pendulous "throatiness." It rises strongly from the shoulders and arches slightly as it tapers to join the head. The shoulders are well laid back forming an angle with the upper arm of approximately 90 degrees which permits the dog to move his forelegs in an easy manner with considerable forward reach. Shoulders are clean-cut and sloping without protrusion and so set that the upper points of the withers are at an angle which permits a wide spring of rib.

Body: The body is short, compact and firmly knit together, giving an impression of strength.

The profile of a Cocker with a deep muzzle and low-set ears.

Standards for the Breed

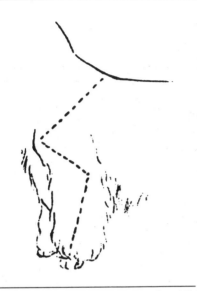

Correct angulation of the Cocker Spaniel's shoulders.

The distance from the highest point of the shoulder blades to the ground is fifteen (15%) per cent or approximately two inches more than the length from this point to the set-on of the tail. Back is strong and sloping evenly and slightly downward from the shoulders to the set-on of the docked tail. Hips are wide and quarters well rounded and muscular. The chest is deep, its lowest point no higher than the elbows, its front sufficiently wide for adequate heart and lung space, yet not so wide as to interfere with the straightforward movement of the forelegs. Ribs are deep and well

sprung. The Cocker Spaniel never appears long and low.

Tail: The docked tail is set on and carried on a line with the topline of the back, or slightly higher; never straight up like a terrier and never so low as to indicate timidity. When the dog is in motion the tail action is merry.

Legs and Feet: Forelegs are parallel, straight, strongly boned and muscular and set close to the body well under the scapulae. When viewed from the side with the forelegs vertical, the elbow is directly below the highest point of the shoulder blade. The pasterns are

Correct angulation of the hindquarters of a Cocker Spaniel.

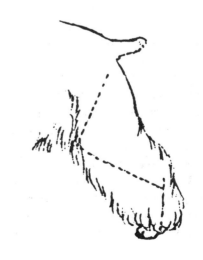

Standards for the Breed

short and strong. The hind legs are strongly boned and muscled with good angulation at the stifle and powerful, clearly defined thighs. The stifle joint is strong and there is no slippage of it in motion or when standing. The hocks are strong, well let down, and when viewed from behind, the hind legs are parallel when in motion and at rest.

Feet: Compact, large, round and firm with horny pads; they turn neither in nor out. Dewclaws on hind legs and forelegs may be removed.

Coat: On the head, short and fine; on the body, medium length, with enough undercoating to give protection. The ears, chest, abdomen and legs are well feathered, but not so excessively as to hide the Cocker Spaniel's true lines and movement or affect his appearance and function as a sporting dog. The *texture* is most important. The coat is silky, flat or slightly wavy, and of a texture which permits easy care. Excessive or curly or cottony textured coat is to be penalized.

Color and Markings:

Black Variety: Solid color black, to include black with tan points. The black should be jet; shadings of brown or liver in the sheen of the

Captions for color photos on pages 17 through 24:

Page 17: Cockers should be groomed and trimmed regularly. A Vince Serbin photo of a parti-colored Cocker Spaniel owned by Doris Fink, White Deer Kennels, Tuckerton, New Jersey. Page 18: The rural setting at the White Deer Kennels is an appropriate environment for raising young Cocker Spaniels. Photo by Vince Serbin. Page 19: A solid chocolate colored Cocker Spaniel. Pages 20-21: A flat wavy coat, not very curly, is characteristic of a good Cocker Spaniel. Photo by Vince Serbin at White Deer Kennels. Page 22: In many kennels, like White Deer, Cockers are kept in cages to protect their coats from wear and tear of running free all the time. Photo by Vince Serbin. Page 23: Cockers adapt well with the family setting, including other animals. Page 24: A lustrous and clean coat is a good indicator of a Cocker's general health. Photo by Vince Serbin at White Deer Kennels.

Captions for color photos on pages 57 through 64:

Page 57: Doris Fink, breeder/owner, proudly displaying her black Cocker Spaniel for this photo by Vince Serbin. Page 58: Both the Dachshund and the Basset Hound shown here have the black and tan color pattern typical of their breed. There are black and tan Cockers too, although slightly different in extent. Page 59: Cockers are hardy. They can be maintained in all seasons of the year outside the home, provided they have some kind of shelter from extreme weather conditions. Photo by Vince Serbin at White Deer Kennels. Page 60: Photos of very young animals are always endearing, as shown here. Page 61: This black Cocker Spaniel bitch, Reverie Reminisce, is owned by Joy Kirkland and Pam Burrow. Page 62: Another Cocker Spaniel, a black and tan, owned by Doris Fink. Photo by Vince Serbin. Page 63: These Cocker Spaniel puppies are still quite young and they fit comfortably in a lady's wicker handbag. Page 64: Sleeping together—a kitten and Cocker Spaniel puppy.

17

Standards for the Breed

coat is not desirable. A small amount of white on the chest and/or throat is allowed, white in any other location shall disqualify.

Any Solid Color Other Than Black: Any solid color other than black and any such color with tan points. The color shall be of a uniform shade, but lighter coloring of the feather is permissible. A small amount of white on the chest and/or throat is allowed, white in any other location shall disqualify.

Parti-Color Variety: Two or more definite, well-broken colors, one of which must be white, including those with tan points; it is

Correct front. Drawing by E. H. Hart.

Correct rear. Drawing by E. H. Hart.

preferable that the tan markings be located in the same pattern as for the tan points in the Black and ASCOB varieties. Roans are classified as parti-colors, and may be of any of the usual roaning patterns. Primary color which is ninety percent (90%) or more shall disqualify.

Tan Points: The color of the tan may be from the lightest cream to the darkest red color and should be restricted to ten percent (10%) or less of the color of the specimen, tan markings in excess of that amount shall disqualify.

In the case of tan points in the Black or ASCOB variety, the markings shall be located as follows:
(1) A clear tan spot over each eye
(2) On the sides of the muzzle and on the cheeks

25

Standards for the Breed

(3) On the undersides of the ears
(4) On all feet and/or legs
(5) Under the tail
(6) On the chest, optional, presence or absence not penalized

Tan markings which are not readily visible or which amount only to traces, shall be penalized. Tan on the muzzle which extends upward, over and joins shall also be penalized. The absence of tan markings in the Black or ASCOB variety in each of the specified locations in an otherwise tan-pointed dog shall disqualify.

Movement: The Cocker Spaniel, though the smallest of the sporting dogs, possesses a typical sporting dog gait. Prerequisite to good movement is balance between the front and rear assemblies. He drives with his strong, powerful rear quarters and is properly constructed in the shoulders and forelegs so that he can reach forward without constriction in a full stride to counterbalance the driving force from the rear. Above all, his gait is coordinated, smooth and effortless. The dog must cover ground with his action and excessive animation should never be mistaken for proper gait.

Height: The ideal height at the withers for an adult dog is 15 inches and for an adult bitch 14 inches. Height may vary one-half inch above or below this ideal. A dog whose height exceeds 15½ inches or a bitch whose height exceeds 14½ inches shall be disqualified. An adult dog whose height is less than 14½ inches or an adult bitch whose height is less than 13½ inches shall be penalized.

Note: Height is determined by a line perpendicular to the ground from the top of the shoulder blades, the dog standing naturally with its forelegs and the lower hind legs parallel to the line of measurements.

DISQUALIFICATIONS
Color and Markings—
   Blacks—White markings except on chest and throat.
   Solid Colors Other Than Black—White markings except on chest and throat.
   Black and Tans—Tan markings in excess of ten (10%) per cent; tan markings not readily visible in the ring, or the absence of tan markings in any of the specified locations; white markings except on chest and throat.
   Parti-Colors—Ninety (90%) per cent or more of primary color; secondary color or colors limited solely to one location.
Height—Males over 15½ inches; females over 14½ inches.

26

The Cocker Spaniel Puppy

Now, assuming that you have decided that this is the right breed for you, there remain the questions of which sex and what age the puppy should be when you purchase him, the preparations to make for his arrival in your home, and the general management of the puppy once he is there.

Sex and Age

This is no place to undertake a "battle of the sexes." Since no dog should run loose, a female, during the brief sex-vulnerable intervals of estrus twice a year, will be chaperoned whenever outdoors; or it is relatively easy to keep her safely confined or to board her with your veterinarian or at a reliable kennel. All her life she can alternate between indoor and outdoor bathroom facilities. A female usually is more gently affectionate, particularly with young children. On the other hand, a male, after he reaches an age to lift his leg, must be let or taken outside to relieve himself four times every single day, no matter what the inconvenience. He may display embarrassing interest in the sex of other dogs he encounters; leave his "calling card" on every post, tree, shrub or hydrant; and although housebroken at home, cannot always be trusted in unfamiliar private or public premises. No one can make this decision for you. "You pays your money, and takes your choice!"

As to age, two and a half to three months is young enough. By that age, a puppy is weaned and independent of his mother's care and company, day or night. He is well adapted to his diet and a convenient meal schedule. He is old enough for vaccinations against distemper and other contagious diseases (in fact, a vaccination program may have already been started for the puppy by his seller), and he is at the most responsive age to begin to understand and heed the lessons of housebreaking. A younger puppy requires frequent attention, almost foster-mothering, which cannot be delegated to children or neglected even for a few hours. A lower price at a lower age is no bargain.

Pet versus Show Prospect

It is well to define in your own mind the purpose for which you want a dog and to convey this to the breeder. A great deal of disappointment and dissatisfaction

The Cocker Spaniel Puppy

can be avoided by a meeting of the minds between seller and buyer.

Although every well-bred, healthy member of the breed makes an ideal companion and pet, actual pet-stock is usually the least expensive of the purebred registered stock. The person who asks for a pet pays a pet-geared price for the animal. Pet stock is least expensive because these dogs are deemed unsuitable for breeding or exhibition in comparison to the standard of perfection for the breed. Generally, only skilled breeders and judges can point out the structural differences between pet- and show-quality dogs.

If you are planning to show your dog, make this clear to the breeder and he will aid you in selecting the best possible specimen of the breed. A show-quality dog may be more expensive than one meant for a pet, but it will be able to stand up to show-ring competition.

The dog seller will help you choose a Cocker Spaniel to suit your expectations of the dog.

Where to Buy Your Puppy

Once you have decided on the particular breed that you want for your pet, your task is to find that one special dog from among several outlets. Buying a well-bred, healthy dog is your foremost concern. By doing a little research in the various dog magazines and newspapers, you can locate the names and addresses of breeders and kennels in your area that are known for breeding quality animals. Your national dog club will also furnish you with addresses of people to contact who are knowledgeable about your chosen breed.

Your local pet shop, although necessarily restricted from carrying all breeds in stock, may sometimes be able to supply quality puppies on demand. Due to the exorbitant amount of space and time needed to properly rear puppies, pet shops generally prefer to assist owners by

The Cocker Spaniel Puppy

supplying all the tools and equipment needed in the raising and training of the puppies. The pet shop proprietor, if unable to obtain a dog for you, can often refer you to a reputable kennel with which he has done business before.

Selection

When you do pick out a puppy as a pet, don't be hasty; the longer you study puppies, the better you will understand them. Make it your transcendent concern to select only one that radiates good health and spirit and is lively on his feet, whose eyes are bright, whose coat shines, and who comes forward eagerly to make and to cultivate your acquaintance. Don't fall for any shy little darling that wants to retreat to his bed or his box, or plays coy behind other puppies or people, or hides his head under your arm or jacket appealing to your protective instinct. *Pick the puppy who forthrightly picks you! The feeling of attraction should be mutual!*

Documents

Now, a little paper work is in order. When you purchase a purebred puppy, you should receive a transfer of ownership, registration material, and other "papers" (a list of the immunization shots, if any, the puppy may have been given; a note on whether or not the puppy has been wormed; a diet and feeding schedule to which the puppy is accustomed) and you are welcomed as a fellow owner to a long, pleasant association with a most lovable pet, and more (news)paper work.

General Preparation

You have chosen to own a particular puppy. You have chosen it very carefully over all other breeds and all other puppies. So before you ever get that puppy home, you will have prepared for its arrival by reading everything you can get your hands on having to do with the management of dogs and puppies. True, you will run into many conflicting opinions, but at least you will not be starting "blind." Read, study, digest. Talk over your plans with your veterinarian, other "dog people," and the seller of your puppy.

When you get your puppy, you will find that your reading and study are far from finished. You've just scratched the surface in your

The Cocker Spaniel Puppy

plan to provide the greatest possible comfort and health for your puppy; and, by the same token, you do want to assure yourself of the greatest possible enjoyment of this wonderful creature. You must be ready for the puppy mentally as well as in the physical requirements.

Transportation

If you take the puppy home by car, protect him from drafts, particularly in cold weather. Wrapped in a towel and carried in the arms or lap of a passenger, the puppy usually will make the trip without mishap. If the pup starts to drool and to squirm, stop the car for a few minutes. Have newspapers handy in case of car-sickness. A

covered carton lined with newspapers provides protection for puppy and car, if you are driving alone. Avoid excitement and unnecessary handling of the puppy on arrival. A puppy is a very small "package" to be making complete change of surroundings and company, and he needs frequent rest and refreshment to renew his vitality.

The First Day and Night

When your puppy arrives in your home, put him down on the floor

A young puppy spends a lot of time getting much-needed rest. Drawing by Elinor Warren.

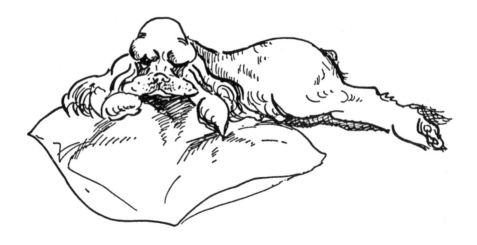

The Cocker Spaniel Puppy

For at least his first few meals, your puppy should get the same food as he received from his previous owner. Drawing by Elinor Warren.

and don't pick him up again, except when it is absolutely necessary. He is a dog, a real dog, and must not be lugged around like a rag doll. Handle him as little as possible, and permit no one to pick him up and baby him. To repeat, *put your puppy on the floor or the ground and let him stay there except when it may be necessary to do otherwise.*

Quite possibly your puppy will be afraid for a while in his new surroundings, without his mother and littermates. Comfort him and reassure him, but don't console him. Don't give him the "oh-you-poor-ittsy-bitsy-puppy" treatment. Be calm, friendly, and reassuring. Encourage him to walk around and sniff over his new home. If it's dark, put on the lights. Let him roam for a few minutes while you and everybody else concerned sit quietly or go about your routine business. Let the puppy come back to you.

Playmates may cause an immediate problem if the new puppy is to be greeted by children or other pets. If not, you can skip this subject. The natural affinity between puppies and children calls for some supervision until a live-and-let-live relationship is established. This applies particularly to a Christmas puppy, when there is more excitement than usual and more chance for a puppy to swallow

The Cocker Spaniel Puppy

something upsetting. It is a better plan to welcome the puppy several days before or after the holiday week. Like a baby, your puppy needs much rest and should not be over-handled. Once a child realizes that a puppy has "feelings" similar to his own, and can readily be hurt or injured, the opportunities for play and responsibilities provide exercise and training for both.

For his first night with you, he should be put where he is to sleep every night—say the kitchen, since its floor can usually be easily cleaned. Let him explore the kitchen to his heart's content; close doors to confine him there. Prepare his food and feed him lightly the first night. Give him a pan with some water in it—not a lot, since most puppies will try to drink the whole pan dry. Give him an old coat or a shirt to lie on. Since a coat or shirt will be strong in human scent, he will pick it out to lie on, thus furthering his feeling of security in the room where he has just been fed.

Housebreaking Helps

Now, sooner or later—mostly sooner—your new puppy is going to "puddle" on the floor. First take a newspaper and lay it on the puddle until the urine is soaked up onto the paper. *Save this paper.* Now take a cloth with soap and water, wipe up the floor and dry it well. Then take the wet paper and place it on a fairly large square of newspapers in a convenient corner. When cleaning up, always keep a piece of wet paper on top of the others. Every time he wants to "squat," he will seek out this spot and use the papers. (This routine is rarely necessary for more than three days.) Now leave your puppy for the night. Quite probably he will cry and howl a bit; some are more stubborn than others on this matter. But let him stay alone for the night. This may seem harsh treatment, but it is the best procedure in the long run. Just let him cry; he will weary of it sooner or later.

Beat Him to the Draw

Puppies, like human infants, wake up at the crack of dawn. So, bright and early, your first job is to take him outdoors for a "business trip." Try to keep him out until he has relieved himself. Then give him his first meal of the day, after which you take him out again. Puppies usually want to relieve themselves first thing in the morning, last thing

The Cocker Spaniel Puppy

at night, after each feeding, and after each nap. To cut down on "mistakes," take him out often for the first few days, until he learns what he is going out for—and keep him near his newspapers. Caution: Do not force him to rely too much on the newspapers or he will get to the point where he will stay out for hours without doing anything and then rush to the papers when he at last is brought indoors.

Housebreaking is a simple thing if done properly. Just cooperate with the inevitable! Anticipate his need before he does. And for the first few mistakes, say nothing to him—especially the first 24 hours. Then, when he misbehaves, point to the error and quietly but firmly say "No" or "Fooey!" Make it decisive. He must know he has done wrong, but he must *not* be scared to death. And under no circumstance must he be slapped, yelled at, or stamped at. Just a brisk "Fooey" or "No." Work things in such a way that he doesn't get a chance to misbehave.

Collar and Leash Training

Now as to general management, immediately put on him a small leather collar and have a leash to go with it. He probably won't notice the collar at all; but if he does, and seems to fight it, let him fight it and pay no attention. He'll get used to it quickly. Leave it on all the time. Whenever he goes outside, snap a leash onto the collar. City or country, always take your dog out with collar and leash. This is his first taste of discipline. And discipline is not punishment—it is training!

All training is done on the leash. He may buck and plunge a bit at first, finding himself unable to run around at will. Hold the leash

1. Limited choke. 2. Pliable leash, six feet long. 3. Chain choke collar. 4. Wooden dumbbell. 5. Long leash.

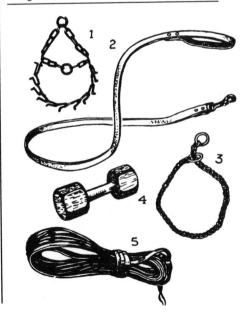

firmly, but let it "give" a lot for the first few days. Do not start him off with the chain collar. Such a collar is ideal later, but it is painful and even dangerous on a young puppy. Gradually teach him to walk quietly on the leash, always on your left side. Hold the leash in such a way to prevent him from running ahead of you or crossing your path. By all means, start his leash- and-collar work as soon as you get him. Don't start his formal training until he is five or six months old, or maybe a little older, depending on the dog himself. Meanwhile, he is learning what "No" means, and he is learning to come when called. Always speak his name first, followed by the command "Come." And make it a command, but slap your knees to encourage him at first. Study your training book now, even though you won't start regular training for months.

Riding in the Car

Start your puppy off right in the car. He will probably have to be boosted in the first few times. Let him sit on the floor. Take him only on short trips for awhile. If the excitement or motion of riding makes him sick, he will begin to drool heavily. When you see this, stop the car and take him out. Let him walk around on the leash a bit—say five or ten minutes. Then put him back in the car and start off again. For several weeks, go for short trips only and make the trips frequent. The younger the puppy, usually the sooner he learns to like driving and the less he is concerned with it.

Take your puppy everywhere—streets, stores—everywhere. Do it in easy stages, but get him accustomed to all sorts of strange sights, sounds, and smells. Thus, when he is mature, he will go anywhere with perfect poise.

Encourage him, too, to stand quietly and be patted by strangers. Be careful that he doesn't learn to dislike children, as sometimes happens with dogs of all breeds, because of rough handling on the part of the children. Let one or two children take him for a walk on his leash once in a while. Let them feed him some special treat as they take him out.

Introducing New Situations

In general, either lead your puppy or encourage him to take the initiative in all new situations. Don't

The Cocker Spaniel Puppy

ever "push" him into them. You will get nowhere and may end up spoiling the dog.

With you and your family, observe the same procedures. Let the dog make the move. Encourage him to sit or lie quietly with the family. Let the dog develop into a sensible, normal dog. Don't fuss with him constantly.

Do not misunderstand the instruction not to make a fuss over the puppy. This does not mean you should bring up your dog in a harsh, strict manner. A dog has a limitless reservoir of love and affection and devotion for those he knows and loves. Sure, play with him. Sure, roughhouse with him, but don't make an addlepated ninny out of him by constantly fooling or talking with him. If there is anything worse than a spoiled child, it's a spoiled dog. Both are a pain in the neck to all concerned. So bring up your puppy to be a friendly, well-mannered, happy, healthy dog. If he doesn't "get around," how can he know how to act under all circumstances? So take him around. Start his training early.

To Spay or Not to Spay

To spay a female dog (past tense, *spayed)* is to remove both ovaries from the dog surgically, thus rendering it impossible for the dog ever to have puppies or periods of "heat," or "season." And make no mistake about it, this is major surgery to be performed only by a graduate, licensed veterinarian. However, in his hands, the practice of spaying is quite generally used and is considered a routine operation. The risk involved is almost zero, assuming that the dog is of correct age and is in excellent health and condition.

Needless to say, there is considerable difference of opinion on spaying. "Spay and spoil your female" is the contention of those who are opposed, although just how the female is "spoiled" is not readily apparent. The opponents will tell you that the spayed female becomes sluggish, dull, has no pep or joy in life, gets enormously fat, and wants only to eat and sleep. It is further alleged that the spayed female is rendered stupid and unable to learn anything.

Now, among old-timers in the dog game, there is a very strong conviction that the female is a far better companion and housedog than the male, and the best housedog and companion is a spayed female. These experienced dog keepers have never seen a fat, stupid spayed female; and they firmly believe that spaying in no way affects the dog's personality or characteristic joy in living. Granted, there is a tendency to get fat, but this situation is easily regulated by proper feeding.

To anyone not interested in breeding dogs but who wants a fine companion and housedog, the spayed female has no superior. Always beautiful anyway, she is keen, smart, and lively.

Special Care for the Brood Bitch

If your female is to be used as a breeding animal, there are certain topics to be covered in the management of the female during her periods of heat.

The female usually comes in heat for the first time between the ages of seven and 12 months. And allowing for some variations in individual dogs, the female will come in heat roughly twice a year, once in the spring and once in the fall, or thereabouts.

The onset of the heat period is marked by a slight discharge of dark red blood from the vulva, or external genital organ, of the female. With this discharge, odorless to humans, comes a gradual swelling and enlargement of the vulva, along with an increased flow of blood, until the ninth or tenth day, at which time the vulva is quite enlarged and the flow has begun to be pinkish or amber colored. The discharge gradually pales out and decreases during the third week. But while the heat period is usually considered to be three weeks, it is much safer to count it a month in duration.

If you live in the city, the heat period will cause you little if any inconvenience, since, in the city, dogs are more apt to be leashed or more carefully controlled than dogs in the suburbs and country. But the safe rule, to guard against accidental breeding, is to keep your female always on a lead throughout the entire heat period. As for the droplets of discharge around the house, they are odorless and may easily be removed by wiping with a damp cloth.

In the country or suburbs, you may have somewhat of a problem. Again, take your female outside only on a leash and keep her close beside you. If possible, walk her a little way from the house to relieve herself, keeping a sharp lookout for visiting males. Some males are extremely fast operators; and unless

Grooming Your Cocker Spaniel

you are very careful, especially from the seventh or eighth day on, you may have an unwanted breeding before you know it. In this instance, once such a breeding has begun, there is absolutely nothing you can do about it. Attempted separation of the two animals will result in serious injury to both. However, should you have such bad luck, immediately take your female to your veterinarian. Sometimes he can prevent a litter of mutts.

Indoors, continue your caution. Along about the eleventh or twelfth day, your female may sneak outside if not watched, and she is sure to run into a group of waiting males. Keep her under lock and key for a full month!

There are various preparations on the market which allegedly discourage male dogs from hanging around. They are usually liquids with a strong, pungent odor designed to fool the nose of the males. Such a preparation may or may not be reliable; but in either case, do not depend on such a product to relieve you of the duty of vigilantly supervising your female's activities during her estrous cycle.

It is no trick to keep a Cocker's coat in good condition if a few simple and easy practices are followed.

In the first place let us understand that it is very necessary that the skin and coat retain the natural oils nature provides to keep them in good condition. It follows then, that a dog should not be bathed frequently. Once a month is ample, and once in three months is preferable.

Bathing

Use tepid water, an ordinary hose spray that fastens to the bathtub faucet, and only those soaps specifically designed for use in bathing dogs. Soak the dog thoroughly and then shampoo in the soap, massaging vigorously. (Be careful not to get water into the ear canal.) Then rinse until the water comes off the dog perfectly clear and the coat is "squeaky clean." Dry well with two turkish towels. Keep the dog out of drafts until completely dry. That's all there is to bathing.

Grooming, on the other hand, is very important and should be a daily chore. The thought to keep in mind is that the more often the coat is groomed, the easier grooming

Grooming Your Cocker Spaniel

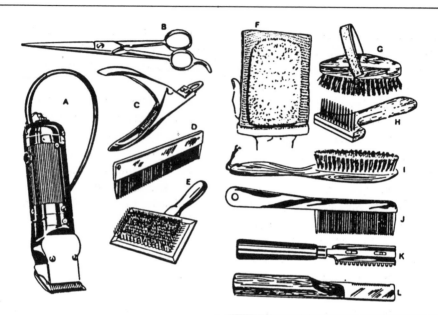

becomes. Once you let dead hair become matted, you have a job on your hands.

Grooming Tools

Your tools are a stiff, steel-toothed comb about seven inches long, a stiff-bristled brush, and, if you like, a slicker brush, which is a flat metal brush with many fine steel bristles and a handle. It resembles a horse's curry comb and is used the same way. It is all right for a quick job, but not as thorough as the comb and brush. Give the coat a good going-over daily, being sure to comb out all dead hair, and your Cocker will always maintain a good appearance and your friends will ask how you keep such a good coat on your dog. Let me emphasize that the grooming chore is a matter of ten or fifteen minutes if done daily; but it's a long job as a once-a-month proposition.

Grooming Your Cocker Spaniel

Trimming Your Cocker

Now let's talk about trimming. As a minimum, if you'll trim the hair around the feet and between the pads, the dog will bring the least dirt into the house. That's easy to do. The only other really necessary attention is the ear canals, and it is essential that they be cleaned out as needed. Use ordinary cotton applicators and alcohol and swab the canals, being careful not to dig too deeply. Then dry with fresh applicators and cotton swabs around the outer ear. If, however, you want to maintain the dog in a barbered trim you will need some tools—and experience. A double-edged instrument, using certain safety razor blades (used with a shaving motion along the lay of the hair), plus a comb, are really the only instruments you need, though you

Steps to trim your Cocker Spaniel: 1. Trim muzzle. 2. Make ears look low set by smoothly trimming skull and cheeks. 3. Trim ears down finely at top. Leave plenty of hair at bottom. Remove hair from inside ears and from neck covered by ear. 4. Trim hair closely from underjaw, throat, and neck. 5. Tidy up brisket. 6. Tidy up front leg feathering with scissors. 7. Clean shoulders where coat is too thick. 8. Clean feathering from tail. 9. Trim hair shape of feet. Do not take hair from between toes. Remove hair from underneath pads. Drawing by Prudence Walker.

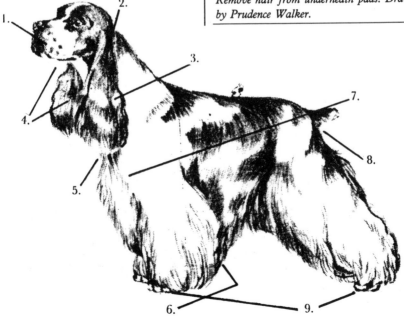

Grooming Your Cocker Spaniel

The head of a female Cocker Spaniel should appear more delicate than that of a male.

From the base of the skull trim the neck, top, and sides, so that it seems to slide into trim, neat shoulders. In front, trim rather closely to a point where the neck disappears into the chest. In general, follow the same procedure over the body and hind legs, removing fuzziness but not chopping the coat. Clean out the hair around and under the tail and the "feather" at the end of the tail. It is assumed that you have already trimmed around the paws.

Trimming does take practice, but it certainly is not beyond average dexterity, and a well-trimmed Cocker is a beauty to behold.

can go on to thinning scissors, clippers, etc.

Starting with the dog's muzzle, take the hair down along both sides, along his underjaw and neck, and along the cheeks and over the skull. Watch your trimming and graduate the short with the longer hair so that no sharp line of demarcation is evident. Start where the ear joins the skull and trim rather closely down along the outer surface for about two inches. Turn the ear up and trim out the tuft of hair under the ear; the idea is to have the ear lie close to the head and to accentuate the length.

The head of a male Cocker Spaniel appears stronger than a female's head.

Feeding

Now let's talk about feeding your dog, a subject so simple that it's amazing there is so much nonsense and misunderstanding about it. Is it expensive to feed a dog? No, it is not! You can feed your dog economically and keep him in perfect shape the year round, or you can feed him expensively. He'll thrive either way, and let's see why this is true.

First of all, remember a dog is a dog. Dogs do not have a high degree of selectivity in their food, and unless you spoil them with great variety (and possibly turn them into poor, "picky" eaters) they will eat almost anything that they become accustomed to. Many dogs flatly refuse to eat nice, fresh beef. They pick around it and eat everything else. But meat—bah! Why? They aren't accustomed to it! They are hounds. They'd eat rabbit fast enough, but they refuse beef because they aren't used to it.

Variety Not Necessary

A good general rule of thumb is forget all about human preferences and don't give a thought to variety. Choose the right diet for your dog and feed it to him day after day, year after year, winter and summer. But what is the right diet?

Hundreds of thousands of dollars have been spent in canine nutrition research. The results are pretty conclusive, so you needn't go into a lot of experimenting with trials of this and that every other week. Research has proven just what your dog needs to eat and to keep healthy.

Dog Food

There are almost as many right diets as there are dog experts, but the basic diet most often recommended is one that consists of a dry food, either meal or kibble form. There are several of these of excellent quality, manufactured by reliable concerns, research tested, and nationally advertised. They are inexpensive, highly satisfactory, and easily available in stores everywhere in containers of five to fifty pounds. Larger amounts cost less per pound, usually.

Feeding

If you have a choice of brands, it is usually safer to choose the better-known one; but even so, carefully read the analysis on the package. Do not choose any food in which the protein level is less than 25 percent, and be sure that this protein comes from both animal *and* vegetable sources. The good dog foods have meat meal, fish meal, liver, and such, plus protein from alfalfa and soybeans, as well as some dried-milk product. Note the vitamin content carefully. See that they are all there in good proportions; and be especially certain that the food contains properly high levels of vitamins A and D, two of the most perishable and important ones. Note the B-complex level, but don't worry about carbohydrate and mineral levels. These substances are plentiful and cheap and not likely to be lacking in a good brand.

The advice given for how to choose a dry food also applies to moist or canned types of dog foods, if you decide to feed one of these.

Having chosen a really good food, feed it to your dog as the manufacturer directs. And once you've started, stick to it. Never change if you can possibly help it. A switch from one meal or kibble-type food can usually be made without too much upset; however, a change will almost invariably give you (and the dog) some trouble.

Fat Important; Meat Optional

While the better dog foods are complete in themselves in every respect, there is one item to add to the food, and that is *fat*—any kind of melted animal fat. It can be lard, bacon, or ham fat or from beef, lamb, pork, or poultry. A grown dog should have at least a tablespoon or two of melted fat added to one feeding a day. If you feed your dog morning and night, give him half of the fat in each feeding.

The addition of meat to this basic ration is optional. There is a sufficient amount of everything your dog needs already in the food, but you may add any meat you wish, say, a half to a quarter of a pound. In adding meat, the glandular meats are best, such as kidneys, pork liver, and veal or beef heart. They are all cheap to buy and are far higher sources of protein than the usual muscle meat humans insist on. Cook these meats slightly or feed them raw. Liver and kidney should be cooked a little and fed sparingly since they are laxative to some dogs. Heart is ideal, raw or cooked. Or you can feed beef, lamb, ocean fish well cooked, and pork.

Feeding

When Supplements Are Needed

Now what about supplements of various kinds, mineral and vitamin, or the various oils? They are all okay to add to your dog's food. However, if you are feeding your dog a correct diet, and this is easy to do, no supplements are necessary unless your dog has been improperly fed, has been sick, or is having puppies. Vitamins and minerals are naturally present in all foods; and to ensure against any loss through processing, they are added in concentrated form to the dog food you use. Except on the advice of your veterinarian, extra and added amounts of vitamins can prove harmful to your dog! The same risk goes with minerals.

Feeding Schedule

When and how much food to give your dog? As to when (except in the instance of puppies which will be taken up later), suit yourself. You may feed two meals per day or the same amount in one single feeding, either morning or night. As to how to prepare the food and how much to give, it is generally best to follow the directions on the food package. Your own dog may want a little more or a little less.

Fresh, cool water should always be available to your dog. This is important to good health throughout his lifetime.

All Dogs Need to Chew

Puppies and young dogs need something with resistance to chew on while their teeth and jaws are developing—for cutting the puppy teeth, to induce growth of the permanent teeth under the puppy teeth, to assist in getting rid of the puppy teeth at the proper time, to help the permanent teeth through the gums, to ensure normal jaw development, and to settle the permanent teeth solidly in the jaws.

The adult dog's desire to chew stems from the instinct for tooth cleaning, gum massage, and jaw exercise—plus the need for an outlet for periodic doggie tensions.

This is why dogs, especially puppies and young dogs, will often destroy property worth hundreds of dollars when their chewing instinct is not diverted from their owner's possessions. And this is why you should provide your dog with something to chew—something that

Feeding

has the necessary functional qualities, is desirable from the dog's viewpoint, and is safe for your dog.

It is very important that dogs not be permitted to chew on anything they can break or on any indigestible thing from which they can bite sizeable chunks. Sharp pieces, such as from a bone which can be broken by a dog, may pierce the intestinal wall and kill. Indigestible things which can be bitten off in chunks, such as from shoes or rubber or plastic toys, may cause an intestinal stoppage (if not regurgitated) and bring painful death, unless surgery is promptly performed.

Strong natural bones, such as 4- to 8-inch lengths of round shin bone from mature beef—either the kind you can get from a butcher or one of the variety available commercially in pet stores—may serve your dog's teething needs if his mouth is large enough to handle them effectively. You may be tempted to give your puppy a smaller bone and he may not be able to break it when you do, but puppies grow rapidly and the power of their jaws constantly increases until maturity. This means that a growing dog may break one of the smaller bones at any time, swallow the pieces, and die painfully before you realize what is wrong.

All hard natural bones are highly abrasive. If your dog is an avid chewer, natural bones may wear away his teeth prematurely; hence, they then should be taken away from your dog when the teething purposes have been served. The badly worn, and usually painful, teeth of many mature dogs can be traced to excessive chewing on natural bones.

Contrary to popular belief, knuckle bones which can be chewed up and swallowed by the dog provide little, if any, useable calcium or other nutriment. They do, however, disturb the digestion of most dogs and cause them to vomit the nourishing food they need.

Dried rawhide products of various types, shapes, sizes, and prices are available on the market and have become quite popular. However, they don't serve the primary chewing functions very well; they are a bit messy when wet from mouthing, and most dogs chew them up rather rapidly—but they have been considered safe for dogs until recently. Now, more and more incidents of death, and near death, by strangulation have been reported to be the result of partially swallowed chunks of rawhide swelling in the throat. More

Feeding

recently, some veterinarians have been attributing cases of acute constipation to large pieces of incompletely digested rawhide in the intestine.

The nylon bones, especially those with natural meat and bone fractions added, are probably the most complete, safe, and economical answer to the chewing need. Dogs cannot break them or bite off sizeable chunks; hence, they are

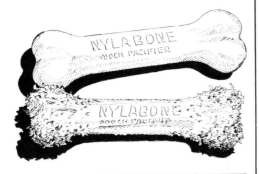

The upper Nylabone has not yet been chewed; the lower Nylabone shows normal signs of wear.

completely safe—and being longer lasting than other things offered for the purpose, they are economical.

Hard chewing raises little bristle-like projections on the surface of the nylon bones—to provide effective interim tooth cleaning and vigorous gum massage, much in the same way your toothbrush does it for you. The little projections are raked off and swallowed in the form of thin shavings, but the chemistry of the nylon is such that they break down in the stomach fluids and pass through without effect.

The toughness of the nylon provides the strong chewing resistance needed for important jaw exercise and effectively aids teething functions, but there is no tooth wear because nylon is non-abrasive. Being inert, nylon does not support the growth of microorganisms; and it can be washed in soap and water or it can be sterilized by boiling or in an autoclave.

Nylabone® is highly recommended by veterinarians as a safe, healthy nylon bone that can't splinter or chip. Nylabone® is frizzled by the dog's chewing action, creating a toothbrush-like surface that cleanses the teeth and massages the gums. Nylabone® and Nylaball® the only chew products made of flavor-impregnated solid nylon, are available in your local pet shop.

Nothing, however, substitutes for periodic professional attention to your dog's teeth and gums, not any more than your toothbrush can do that for you. Have your dog's teeth cleaned by your veterinarian at least once a year (twice a year is better) and he will be healthier, happier, and far more pleasant to live with.

Training

You owe proper training to your dog. The right and privilege of being trained is his birthright; and whether your dog is going to be a handsome, well-mannered housedog and companion, a show dog, or whatever possible use he may be put to, the basic training is always the same—all must start with basic obedience, or what might be called "manners training."

Your dog must come instantly when called and obey the "Sit" or "Down" command just as fast; he must walk quietly at "Heel," whether on or off the lead. He must be mannerly and polite wherever he goes; he must be polite to strangers on the street and in stores. He must be orderly in the presence of other dogs. He must not bark at children on roller skates, motorcycles, or domestic animals. And he must be restrained from chasing cats. It is not a dog's inalienable right to chase cats, and he must be reprimanded for it.

Professional Training

How do you go about this training? Well, it's a very simple procedure, pretty well standardized by now. First, if you can afford the extra expense, you may send your dog to a professional trainer, where in 30 to 60 days he will learn how to be a "good dog." If you enlist the services of a good professional trainer, follow his advice about when to come to see the dog. No, he won't forget you, but too-frequent visits at the wrong time may slow down his training progress. And using a "pro" trainer means you will have to go for some training, too, after the trainer feels your dog is ready to go home. You will have to learn how your dog works, just what to expect of him and how to use what the dog has learned after he is home.

Obedience Training Class

Another way to train your dog (many experienced dog people think this is the best) is to join an obedience-training class right in your own community. There is such a group in nearly every community nowadays. Here you will be working with a group of people who are also just starting out. You will actually be training your own dog, since all work is done under the direction of a head trainer who will make suggestions to you and also tell you when and how to correct your dog's errors. Then, too, working with

Training

such a group, your dog will learn to get along with other dogs. And, what is more important, he will learn to do exactly what he is told to do, no matter how much confusion there is around him or how great the temptation to go his own way.

Write to your national kennel club for the location of a training club or class in your locality. Sign up. Go to it regularly—every session! Go early and leave late! Both you and your dog will benefit tremendously.

Train Him By The Book

The third way of training your dog is by the book. Yes, you can do it this way and do a good job of it too. If you can read and if you're smarter than the dog, you'll do a good job. But in using the book method, select a book, buy it, study it carefully; then study it some more, until the procedures are almost second nature to you. *Then* start your training. But stay with the book and its advice and exercises. Don't start in and then make up a few rules of your own. If you don't follow the book, you'll get into jams you can't get out of by yourself. If after a few hours of short training sessions your dog is

still not working as he should, get back to the book for a study session, because it's *your* fault, not the dog's! The procedures of dog training have been so well systematized that it must be your fault, since literally thousands of fine dogs have been trained by the book.

After your dog is "letter perfect" under all conditions, then, if you wish, go on to advanced training and trick work.

Your dog will love his obedience training, and you'll burst with pride at the finished product! Your dog will enjoy life even more, and you'll enjoy your dog more. And remember—you *owe* good training to your dog!

There are a number of good books that give detailed training information.

Showing

A show dog is a comparatively rare thing. He is one out of several litters of puppies. He happens to be born with a degree of physical perfection that closely approximates the standard by which the breed is judged in the show ring. Such a dog should, at maturity, be able to win or approach his championship in good, fast company at the larger shows. Upon finishing his championship, he is apt to be highly desirable as a breeding animal. As a proven stud, he will automatically command a high price for service.

Showing dogs is a lot of fun—yes, but it is a highly competitive sport. Though all the experts were once beginners, the odds are against a novice. You will be showing against experienced handlers, both pro and amateur, people who have devoted a lifetime to breeding, picking the right ones, and then showing those dogs through to their championships. Moreover, the most perfect dog ever born has faults, and in your hands the faults will be far more evident than with the experienced handler who knows how to minimize his dog's faults. There are but a few points on the sad side of the picture.

The experienced handler, however, was not born knowing the ropes. He learned—*and so can you!* You can if you will put in the same time, study, and keen observation that he did. But it will take time!

Key to Success

First, search for a truly fine show-prospect puppy. Take the puppy home, raise him by the book, and, as carefully as you know how, give him every chance to mature into the dog hoped for. Some dog experts recommend keeping a show-prospect puppy out of big shows, even Puppy Classes, until he is mature. When he is approaching maturity, break him in at match shows (more on these later); after this experience for the dog and you, then go gunning for the big wins at the big shows.

48

Showing

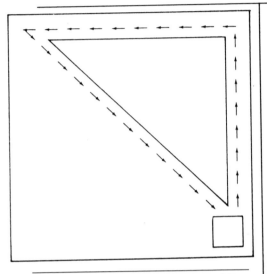

Although there are different patterns to follow when gaiting your dog, this is the one most frequently used.

Next step: read the standard by which the breed is judged. Study it until you know it by heart. Having done this—and while your puppy is at home (where he should be) growing into a fine normal, healthy dog—go to every dog show you can possibly reach. Sit at the ringside and watch the judging. Keep your ears and eyes open. Do your own judging, holding each of those dogs against the standard, which you now know by heart.

In your evaluations, don't start off looking for faults. Look for the virtues—the best qualities. How does a given dog shape up against the standard? Having looked for and noted the virtues, then note the faults and see what prevents a given dog from standing correctly or moving well. Weigh these faults against the virtues, since, ideally, every feature of the dog should contribute to the harmonious whole.

"Ringside Judging"

It's a good practice to make notes on each dog, always holding the dog against the standard. In "ringside judging," forget your personal preference for this or that feature. What does the standard say about it? Watch carefully as the judge places the dogs in a given class. It is difficult from the ringside always to see why number one was placed over the second dog. Try to follow the judge's reasoning. Later try to talk with the judge after he is finished (not every judge will have the time or inclination for this). Ask him questions as to why he placed certain dogs and not others. Listen while the judge explains his placings.

When you're not at the ringside, talk with the fanciers and breeders. Don't be afraid to ask opinions or say that you don't know. You have a lot of listening to do, and it will help you a great deal and speed up

Showing

your personal progress if you are a good listener.

Join the Clubs

You will find it worthwhile to join the national kennel club, which is the governing body for all purebred dogs in a particular country, and to subscribe to its magazine, if one is published. From this national kennel club, you can learn the location of the national breed club (known as the "parent club" for that breed), which you also should join. Being a member of these clubs will afford you the opportunity to get to know other people who share your interests and concerns, to learn more about your breed, and to find out when and where match shows and point shows will be held.

For information regarding sanctioned shows in most English-speaking areas, write to one of the kennel clubs listed below:

American Kennel Club
51 Madison Avenue
New York, NY 10010
USA

Australian Kennel Club
Royal Show Grounds
Ascot Vale, Victoria
Australia

British Kennel Club
1 Clarges Street
London 41Y 8AB
England

Canadian Kennel Club
2150 Bloor Street West
Toronto, Ontario M6S 4V7
Canada

Irish Kennel Club
23 Earlsfort Terrace
Dublin 2
Ireland

Prepare for the Show

The first thing you must do to prepare for a show is to find out the dates and rules of the show you intend to attend. Write to the national kennel club and get a copy of their show dates and rules (and rules for obedience competition or field trials or whatever type of competition you are interested in).

You also must teach your dog and yourself some basics of dog showing. You must learn to "stack" your dog, and your dog must learn to stay in this show stance whenever required to do so. Your dog must learn to accept being examined by a stranger (in other words, the judge at the show). You will have to learn how to gait your dog, and your dog must learn how to move properly at your side.

Enter Match Shows

Match shows differ from regular shows only in that no championship points are given. These shows are especially designed to launch young dogs (and young handlers) on a show career.

With the ring deportment you have watched at big shows firmly in mind and practice, enter your dog in as many match shows as you can. When in the ring, you have two jobs. One is to see to it that your dog is always being seen to best advantage. The other job is to keep your eye on the judge to see what he may want you to do next. Watch only the judge and your dog. Be quick and be alert; do exactly as the judge directs. Don't speak to him except to answer his questions. If he does something you don't like, don't say so. And don't irritate the judge (and everybody else) by constantly talking and fussing with your dog.

In moving about the ring, remember to keep clear of dogs beside you or in front of you. Many dog fanciers feel that you should *not* show your dog in a regular point show until he is at least close to maturity and after both you and he have had time to perfect ring manners and poise in the match shows.

Point Shows

Point shows are for purebred dogs registered with the club that is sanctioning the show. Each dog is entered in the show class which is appropriate for his age, sex, and previous show record. The show classes usually include Puppy, Novice, Bred-by-Exhibitor, American-bred, and Open; and there may also be a Veterans Class and Brace and Team Classes, among others.

There also may be a Junior Showmanship Class, a competition for youngsters. Young people between the ages of 10 and 16, inclusively, compete to see who best handles their dog, rather than to see which dog is best, as is done in the other classes.

For a complete discussion of show dogs, dog shows, and showing a dog, read *Successful Dog Show Exhibiting* by Anna Katherine Nicholas (T.F.H. Publications, Inc.).

Breeding

So you have a female dog and you want to breed her for a litter of puppies. Wonderful idea—very simple—lots of fun—make a lot of money. Well, it *is* a wonderful idea, but stop right there. It's not very simple—and you won't make a lot of money. Having a litter of puppies to bring up is

The external skeletal parts of a dog: 1. Cranium. 2. Cervical vertebra. 3. Thoracic vertebra. 4. Rib. 5. Lumber vertebra. 6. Ilium. 7. Femur. 8. Fibula. 9. Tibia. 10. Tarsus. 11. Metatarsus. 12. Phalanges. 13. Phalanges. 14. Ulna. 15. Radius. 16. Humerus. 17. Scapula.

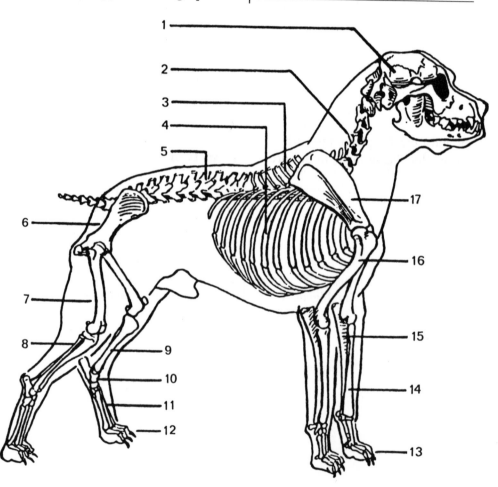

Breeding

hard, painstaking, thoughtful work; and only a few people regard such work as fun.

Breed Better Dogs

Bear in mind this very important point: Being a dog breeder is not just breeding dear Tillie to that darned good-looking male down the street. Would that it were that simple! Such a breeding will undoubtedly produce puppies. But that is not all you want. When you breed your female, it is only after the most careful planning—with every effort being made to be sure that the resulting puppies will be even better than the parent dogs (that they will come even closer to the standard than the parent animals) and that all the puppies will have good homes. Any fool can breed a litter of puppies; but only a careful, thoughtful, intelligent person can breed a litter of better puppies of your breed of dog. That must be your goal in breeding!

You can become a good novice breeder if you truly love the breed and are seriously concerned with the past, present, and future of the breed. You will breed your female only according to established scientific principles. Your personal

sentiments have no place in the careful planning that goes on before you actually breed your female. The science of mammalian genetics is not a precise science like, say, mathematics. And the extensive reading you will do on the science (or art) of breeding dogs before you start to choose a stud will give you some idea of the variable factors you will be dealing with. It is a vast subject; but with the few brief pointers given here and additional reading and study, you can at least start on the right track.

Plan It on Paper

The principles of animal breeding are the same, whether the subjects be beef cattle, poultry, or dogs. To quote a cattle breeder, every breeding is first made "on paper" and later in the barnyard. In other words, first the blood strains of the animals are considered as to what goes well with what, so far as recorded ancestry is concerned. Having worked this out, the two animals to be mated must be studied and compared. If one does not excel where the other is lacking, at least in most points, then the paper planning must start over again and different animals be considered.

Breeding

With your own dog, there are several "musts" that are really axioms. First, breed only the best to the best. Two inferior animals will produce nothing but inferior animals, as surely as night follows day. To breed an inferior dog to another inferior one is a crime against the breed. So start by breeding the best to the best. And here again, an accurate knowledge of the standard is essential to know just what is best.

"Compensation" Breeding

No perfect dog has yet been whelped. Your female may be a winning show dog. She may be a champion. But she does have faults. In breeding her to a fine male, you must consider "compensation" breeding. She must compensate for his shortcomings and he for hers. For example, your female may be ideal in most respects but have faulty feet. So the male you choose, however ideal in other respects, *must* have ideal feet, as had his sire and dam too. In this way you may overcome the foot faults in your female's puppies.

This same principle applies to the correction of faults in any section of either male or female. But, you say, my dog has a pedigree as long as your arm. Must be good! Sad but true, a pedigree will not necessarily produce good puppies. A pedigree is no more—and no less—than your dog's recorded ancestry. Yes, you must know what dogs are in your dog's pedigree, but the most important point is, Were they good dogs? What were their faults and virtues? And to what degree did these dogs transmit these faults and virtues?

Breeding Methods

Now you may have heard that "like begets like." This is true and it is also false! Likes can beget likes only when both parent animals have the same likeness through generations of both family lines. The only way known to "fix" virtues and to eliminate faults is to mate two dogs of fairly close relationship bloodwise, two dogs which come from generations of likes and are family-related in their likeness. In this way you may ensure a higher and regular percentage of puppies which can be expected to mature into adults free at least from major faults under the standard. The likes must have the same genetic inheritance.

Through this "family" breeding, or line-breeding, correct type is set

Care of Mother and Family

and maintained. If both family lines are sound to begin with, family breeding and even close inbreeding (mating closely related dogs such as father and daughter) will merely improve the strain—but only in skilled hands. "Outcrossing" is mating dogs of completely different bloodlines with no, or only a few, common ancestors; it is used when undesirable traits begin to haunt closer breeding or when the breeder wants to bring in a specific trait or feature. The finest dogs today are the result of just such breeding methods. Study, expert advice, and experience will enable you, a novice, to follow these principles. So in your planning, forget the old nonsense about idiots and two-headed monsters coming from closely related parents.

Then, too, in your planning and reading, remember that intangible virtues, as well as physical ones, are without doubt inherited, as are faults in those intangibles. For example, in breeding bird dogs, where "nose sense" is of greatest importance, this factor can to a degree be fixed for future generations of puppies when the ancestors on both sides have the virtue of "nose sense." Just so, other characteristics of disposition or temperament can be fixed.

Let us assume that you have selected the right stud dog for your female and that she has been bred. In some 58 to 63 days, you will be presented with a nice litter of puppies. But there are a number of things to be gone over and prepared for in advance of the whelping date.

Before your female was bred, she was, of course, checked by your veterinarian and found to be in good condition and free from worms of any sort. She was in good weight but not fat. Once your female has been bred, you should keep your veterinarian informed of your female's progress; and when the whelping is imminent, your vet should be informed so that he can be on call in case any problems arise.

There's an old saying, "A litter should be fed from the day the bitch is bred," and there is a world of truth in it. So from the day your female is bred right up to the time the puppies are fully weaned, the mother's food is of the greatest importance. Puppies develop very rapidly in their 58 to 63 days of gestation, and their demands on the mother's system for nourishment are great. In effect, you are feeding your female and one to six or more other dogs, all at the same time.

Care of Mother and Family

The color captions for pages 57-64 can be found on page 16.

Additions to Regular Diet

For the first 21 days, your female will need but few additions to her regular diet. Feed her as usual, except for the addition of a small amount of "pot " or cottage cheese. This cheese, made from sour milk, is an ideal, natural source of added protein, calcium, and phosphorus—all essential to the proper growth of the unborn litter. Commercial vitamin-mineral supplements are unnecessary if the mother is fed the proper selection of natural foods.

Most commercial supplements are absolutely loaded with mineral calcium. You will usually find that the bulk of the contents is just plain calcium, a cheap and plentiful substance. Some dog experts believe, however, that calcium from an animal source like cheese is far more readily assimilated, and it is much cheaper besides. At any rate, do not use a commercial supplement without consulting your veterinarian and telling him the diet your dog is already getting.

Increase Food Intake

Along about the fifth week, the litter will begin to show a little, and now is the time to start an increase in food intake, not so much in bulk as in nutritive value. The protein content of your female's regular diet should be increased by the addition of milk products (cottage cheese, for example) meat (cooked pork liver, raw beef or veal heart, or some other meat high in protein), and eggs (either the raw yolk alone or, if the white is used, the egg should be cooked). Meanwhile, high-calorie foods should be decreased. The meat, cut into small pieces or ground, can be added to the basic ration. Mineral and vitamin supplements and cod-liver oil or additional fat also can be given to the female at this point, if your veterinarian so recommends.

Feed Several Times A Day

By now, your female is but a few weeks away from her whelping date, and the growing puppies are compressing her internal organs to an uncomfortable degree. She will have to relieve herself with greater frequency now. The stomach, too, is being compressed, so try reducing

56

Care of Mother and Family

the basic ration slightly and at the same time increasing the meats, eggs, and milk products. Feed several small meals per day in order to get in the proper, stepped-up quantity of food without causing the increased pressure of a single large meal. The bitch should be fed generously, but she should not be allowed to become overweight.

Regular Exercise Important

A great deal of advice has been given by experts on keeping the female quiet from the day she is bred all through the pregnancy. Such quiet, however, is not natural and it cannot be enforced. Naturally, the female should not be permitted to go in for fence jumping; but she will be as active as ever during the first few weeks and gradually she will, of her own accord, slow down appropriately, since no one knows quite as much about having puppies as the dog herself—up to a point. But see to it that your female has plenty of gentle exercise all along. She'll let you know when she wants to slow down.

The color captions for pages 57-64 can be found on page 16.

Treat her normally, and don't let her be the victim of all the sentimentality that humans with impending families are heir to.

Whelping Imminent

About the morning of the 58th day or shortly thereafter, your female, who now looks like an outsize beer barrel, will suddenly refuse her food. She may drink water, however. If you have been observant as things progressed, your hand, if not your eye, will tell you that the litter has dropped. The female now has a saggy abdomen, and this is the tip-off that whelping will occur soon, usually well within the next 24 hours. As the actual whelping hour approaches, the mother will become increasingly restless. She will seek out dark places like closets. She will scratch at the floor and wad up rugs as if making a bed. She is pretty miserable right now, so be gently sympathetic with her but *not maudlin!*

Get her to stay in the whelping box you have had prepared for several days. The floor of the box should be covered with an old blanket or towel so that she will feel comfortable there. When the whelping starts, replace the bedding

Care of Mother and Family

with newspapers; these can be replaced as they get scratched up or soiled.

The whelping box should be located in a warm, not hot, place free from drafts. The area should also be fairly quiet. You may, if you wish, confine her to the box by hitching her there with a leash to a hook three or four feet off the floor so she won't get twisted up in it. But when actual whelping starts, take off both leash and collar. Then, get yourself a chair and prepare for an all-night vigil. Somehow puppies always seem to be born at night, and the process is good for 12 to 14 hours usually.

Labor Begins

Stay with her when she starts to whelp, you and one other person she knows well and who is an experienced breeder. No audience, please! A supply of warm water, old turkish towels, and plenty of wiping rags are in order at this point.

When labor commences, the female usually assumes a squatting position, although some prefer to lie down. The first puppy won't look much like a puppy to you when it is fully expelled from the female. It will be wrapped in a dark, membranous sac, which the mother will tear open with her teeth, exposing one small, noisy pup—very wet. Let the mother lick the puppy off and help to dry it. She will also bite off the navel cord. This may make the puppy squeal, but don't worry, mama is not trying to eat her pup. The mother may eat a few of the sacs; this is normal. When she is through cleaning the puppy off, pick up the puppy and gently but firmly give it a good rubbing with a turkish towel. Do this in full sight of the mother and close enough so that she will not leave her whelping box.

When the puppy is good and dry and "squawking" a bit, place it near the mother or in a shallow paper box close to the mother so she can see it but will not step on it when she becomes restless with labor for the second puppy. If the room temperature is lower than 70 degrees, place a hot-water bottle wrapped in a towel near the puppies. Be sure to keep the water changed and warm so the puppies aren't lying on a cold water bottle. Constant warmth is essential.

Most dogs are easy whelpers, so you need not anticipate any trouble. Just stay with the mother, more as an observer than anything else. The experienced breeder who is keeping you company, or your vet, should handle any problems that arise.

Care of Mother and Family

Post-natal Care

When you are reasonably certain that the mother has finished whelping, have your veterinarian administer the proper amount of obstetrical pituitrin. This drug will induce labor again, thus helping to expel any retained afterbirth or dead puppy.

Inspect your puppies carefully. Rarely will any deformities be found; but if there should be any, make a firm decision to have your veterinarian destroy the puppy or puppies showing deformities.

During and after whelping, the female is very much dehydrated, so at frequent intervals she should be offered lukewarm milk or meat soup, slightly thickened with well-soaked regular ration. She will relish liquids and soft foods for about 24 hours, after which she will go back to her regular diet. But be sure she has a constant supply of fresh water available. Feed her and keep her water container outside the whelping box.

After all of the puppies have been born, the mother might like to go outside for a walk. Allow her this exercise. She probably won't want to be away from her puppies more than a minute or two.

The puppies will be blind for about two weeks, with the eyes gradually opening up at that time.

The little pups will be quite active and crawl about over a large area. Be sure that all of the puppies are getting enough to eat. If the mother sits or stands, instead of lying still to nurse, the probable cause is scratching from the puppies nails. You can remedy this by clipping them, as you do hers.

Weaning Time

Puppies can usually be completely weaned at six weeks of age, although you can start to feed them at three weeks. They will find it easier to lap semi-solid food. At four weeks they should be given four meals a day, and soon they will do without their mother entirely. Start them on mixed dog food, or leave it with them in a dish for self-feeding. Don't leave water with them all the time; at this age everything is to play with and they will use it as a wading pool. They can drink all they need if it is offered several times a day, after meals.

As the puppies grow up, the mother will go into the box only to nurse them, first sitting up and then standing. The periods of time between the mother's visits to the box will gradually lengthen, until it is no longer necessary for her to nurse the pups.

Health and Disease

First, don't be frightened by the number of health problems that a dog might have over the course of his life-time. The majority of dogs never have any of them. Don't become a dog-hypochondriac. All dogs have days when they feel lazy and want to lie around doing nothing. For the few problems that you might be concerned about, remember that your veterinarian is your dog's best friend. When you first get your puppy, select a veterinarian whom you have faith in. He will get to know your dog and will be glad to have you consult him for advice. A dog needs little medical care, but that little is essential to his good health and well-being. He needs a proper diet given at regular hours; clean, roomy housing; daily exercise; companionship and love; frequent grooming; and regular check-ups by your veterinarian.

Using a Thermometer and Giving Medicines

Almost every serious ailment shows itself by an increase in the dog's body temperature. If your dog acts lifeless, looks dull-eyed, and gives the impression of illness,

The proper way to give a pill or tablet.

check his temperature by using a rectal thermometer made of either plastic or glass. Hold the dog securely, insert the thermometer (which you have lubricated with petroleum jelly), and take a reading. The average normal temperature for your dog will be 101.5°F. Excitement may raise the temperature slightly; but any rise of

The proper way to give liquid medication.

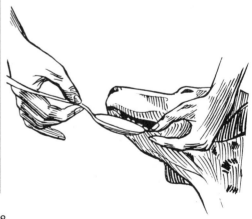

Health and Disease

more than a few points is cause for alarm, and your vet should be consulted.

Giving medicines to your dog is not really difficult. In order to administer a liquid medication, do not open the dog's mouth. Instead, form a pocket by pulling out the lower lip at the corner of the mouth; pour the medicine in with a spoon; hold the head only very slightly upward. (If the head is held too high, the medicine may enter the windpipe instead of the passage to the stomach, thus choking the dog.) With agitated animals, medicine can still be given by this method, even though the dog's mouth is held shut with a tape or a muzzle.

In order to administer a pill or tablet, raise your dog's head slightly and open his mouth. (Using one hand, grasp the cheeks of the dog, and then press inward. The pressure of the lips pushed against the teeth will keep the mouth open). With the other hand, place the pill or tablet far back on the middle of the tongue. Quickly remove your hand from the dog's cheeks; hold the dog's mouth closed (but not too tightly), and gently massage his throat. You can tell the medicine has been swallowed when the tip of the dog's tongue shows between his front teeth.

A Vaccination Schedule

Prevention is the key word for many dog diseases, and the best prevention is a series of vaccinations administered by your veterinarian. Such contagious diseases as distemper, hepatitis, parainfluenza, leptospirosis, rabies, and canine parvovirus can be virtually eliminated by strictly following a vaccination schedule.

Distemper is probably the most virulent of all dog diseases. Young dogs are most susceptible to it, although it may affect dogs of all ages. The dog will lose his appetite, seem depressed, feel chilled, and run a fever. Often he will have a watery discharge from his eyes and nose. Unless treated promptly, the disease goes into advanced stages with infections of the lungs, intestines, and nervous system; and dogs that recover may be left with some impairment such as paralysis, convulsions, a twitch, or some other defect, usually spastic in nature. The best protection against this is very early inoculation with a series of permanent shots and a booster shot each year thereafter.

Hepatitis is a viral disease spread by contact. The initial symptoms of drowsiness, vomiting, great thirst, loss of appetite, and a high temperature closely resemble those

69

Health and Disease

of distemper. These symptoms are often accompanied by swellings of the head, neck, and abdomen. The disease strikes quickly; death may occur in just a few hours. Protection is afforded by injection with a vaccine.

Parainfluenza is commonly called "kennel cough." Its main symptom is coughing; and since it is highly contagious, it can sweep through an entire kennel in just a short period of time. A vaccination is a dog's best protection against this respiratory disease.

Leptospirosis is caused by bacteria that live in stagnant or slow-moving water. It is carried by rats and mice, and infection is begun by the dog licking substances contaminated by the urine or feces of infected animals. The symptoms are diarrhea and a yellowish-brownish discoloration of the jaws, tongue, and teeth, caused by an inflammation of the kidneys. This disease can be cured if caught in time, but it is best to ward it off with a vaccine which your veterinarian can administer.

Rabies is an acute disease of the dog's central nervous system. It is spread by infectious saliva transmitted by the bite of an infected animal. Rabies is generally manifested in one or the other of two groups of symptoms, and the symptoms usually appear within five days. The first is "furious rabies," in which the dog exhibits changes in his personality. The dog becomes hypersensitive and runs at and bites everything in sight. Eventually, the animal's lower jaw becomes paralyzed and hangs down; he walks with a stagger and saliva drips from his mouth. The second syndrome is referred to as "dumb rabies" and is characterized by the dog's walking in a bearlike manner, head down. The lower jaw is paralyzed, and the dog is unable to bite. Outwardly, it may seem as though he has a bone caught in his throat.

Even if your pet should be bitten by a rabid dog or other animal, he probably can be saved if you get him to the veterinarian in time for a series of injections. However, after the symptoms have appeared, no cure is possible. Remember that an annual rabies inoculation is almost certain protection against rabies. If you suspect that your dog or some other animal has rabies, notify your local health department. A rabid animal is a danger to all who come near him.

Canine parvovirus is a highly contagious viral disease that attacks the intestinal tract, white blood cells, and less frequently the heart muscle. It is believed to spread through dog-to-dog contact (the

Health and Disease

specific source of infection being the fecal matter of infected dogs), but it can also be transmitted from place to place on the hair and feet of infected dogs and by contact with contaminated cages, shoes, and the like. It is particularly hard to overcome because it is capable of existing in the environment for many months under varying conditions, unless strong disinfectants are used.

The symptoms are vomiting, fever, diarrhea (often blood-streaked), depression, loss of appetite, and dehydration. Death may occur in only two days. Puppies are hardest hit, with the virus being fatal to 75 percent of the puppies that contact it. Older dogs fare better; the disease is fatal to only two to three percent of those afflicted.

The best preventive measure for parvovirus is vaccination administered by your veterinarian. Precautionary measures individual pet owners can take include disinfecting the kennel and other areas where the dog is housed. One part sodium hypochlorite solution (household bleach) to 30 parts of water will do the job efficiently. Keep the dog from coming into contact with the fecal matter of other dogs when walking or exercising your pet.

Internal Parasites

There are four common internal parasites that may infect your dog. These are roundworms, hookworms, whipworms, and tapeworms. The first three can be diagnosed by laboratory examination; the presence of tapeworms is determined by seeing segments in the stool or attached to the hair around the tail. Do not under any circumstances attempt to worm your dog without the advice of your veterinarian. After first determining what type of worm or worms are present, he will advise you of the best method of treatment.

A dog or puppy in good physical condition is less susceptible to worm infestation than a weak dog. Proper sanitation and a nutritious diet help in preventing worms. One of the best preventive measures is to always have clean, dry bedding for

Adult whipworms are between two and three inches long, and the body of each worm is no thicker than a heavy sewing needle.

Health and Disease

your dog. This will diminish the possibility of reinfection due to flea or tick bites.

Heartworm infestation in dogs is passed by mosquitoes and can be a life-threatening problem. Dogs with the disease tire easily, have difficulty breathing, cough, and may lose weight despite a hearty appetite. If caught in the early stages, the disease can be effectively treated; however, the administration of daily preventive medicine throughout the spring, summer, and fall months is strongly advised. Your veterinarian must first take a blood sample from your dog to test for the presence of the disease. If the dog is heartworm-free, pills or liquid medicine can be prescribed that will protect against any infestation.

Above: Red mange mite.

Below: The common dog flea.

A female dog tick that is gorged with blood.

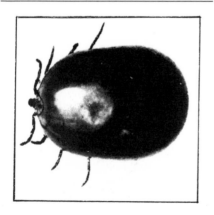

Below: The under side of a sarcoptic mange mite.

Health and Disease

External Parasites

Fleas and ticks are the two most common external parasites that can trouble a dog. Along with the general discomfort and irritation that they bring to a dog, these parasites can infest him with worms and disease. The flea is a carrier of tapeworm and may act as an intermediate host for heartworm. The tick can cause dermatitis and anemia, and it may also be a carrier of Rocky Mountain spotted fever and canine babesiasis, a blood infection. If your dog becomes infested with fleas, he should be treated with a medicated dip bath or some other medication recommended by your vet. Ticks should be removed with great care;

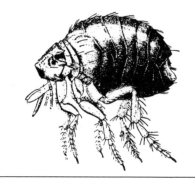

A sticktight flea.

you must be certain that the head of the tick is not left in the dog—this could be a source of infection.

Two types of mange, sarcoptic and follicular, are also caused by parasites. The former is by far the more common and results in an intense irritation, causing violent scratching. Close examination will reveal small red spots which become filled with pus. This is a highly

A female tick.

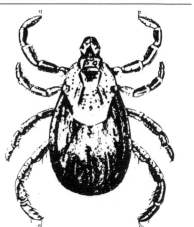

A male tick.

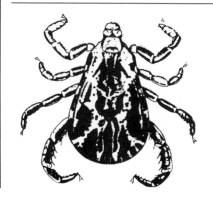

Health and Disease

contagious condition, and any dog showing signs of the disease should be isolated. Consult your veterinarian for the proper treatment procedures. Follicular mange is very much harder to cure; but fortunately, it is much rarer and less contagious. This disease will manifest itself as bare patches appearing in the skin, which becomes thickened and leathery. A complete cure from this condition is only rarely effected.

Other Health Problems

Hip dysplasia is an often crippling condition more prevalent in large

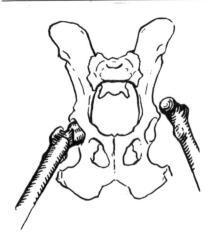

A dislocation of the upper leg bone. Dislocations should be immediately attended to by your vet.

breeds than in small, but it has occurred in almost every breed. The cause is not known absolutely, though it is believed to be hereditary, and as yet there is no known cure. The condition exists in varying degrees of severity. In general, hip dysplasia can be described as a poor fit between the two bones of the hip joint and is caused by a malformation of one or the other. The condition causes stiffness in the hindlegs, considerable pain in the more severe cases, and difficulty of movement. It generally manifests itself in puppyhood and can be noticed by the time the young dog is two months old. If hip dysplasia is suspected, the dog should be x-rayed; and if afflicted, it should not be used for breeding. When the pain is severe and continual, euthanasia is occasionally recommended, though medication is available to control the pain and allow the dog to move with more ease.

Coughs, colds, bronchitis, and pneumonia are respiratory diseases that may affect the dog. Being subjected to cold or a draft after a bath, sleeping near an air conditioner or in the path of a fan, or resting near a radiator can cause respiratory ailments. The symptoms are similar to those in humans;

Health and Disease

however, the germs of these diseases are different and do not affect both dogs and humans, so they cannot be infected by each other. Treatment is much the same as for a child with the same type of illness. Keep the dog warm, quiet, and well fed. Your veterinarian has antibiotics and other remedies to help the dog recover.

Eczema is a disease that occurs most often in the summer months and affects the dog down the back, especially just above the root of the tail. It should not be confused with mange, as it is not caused by a parasite. One of the principle causes of eczema is improper nutrition, which makes the dog susceptible to disease. Hot, humid weather promotes the growth of bacteria, which can invade a susceptible dog and thereby cause skin irritation and lesions. It is imperative that the dog gets relief from the itching that is symptomatic of the disease, as self-mutilation by scratching will only help to spread the inflammation. Antibiotics may be necessary if a bacterial infection is, indeed, present.

Moist eczema, commonly referred to as "hot spots," is a rapidly appearing skin disease that produces a moist infection. Spots appear very suddenly and may spread rapidly in a few hours, infecting several parts of the body. These lesions are generally bacterially infected and are extremely itchy, which will cause the dog to scratch frantically and further damage the afflicted areas. Vomiting, fever, and an enlargement of the lymph nodes may occur. The infected areas must be clipped to the skin and thoroughly cleaned. Your veterinarian will prescribe an anti-inflammatory drug and antibiotics, as well as a soothing emollient to relieve itching.

The *eyes*, because of their sensitivity, are prone to injury and infection. Dogs that spend a great deal of time outdoors in heavily wooded areas may return from an exercise excursion with watery eyes, the result of brambles and high weeds scratching them. The eyes may also be irritated by dirt and other foreign matter. Should your dog's eyes appear red and watery, a mild solution can be mixed at home for a soothing washing. Your veterinarian will be able to tell you what percentage of boric acid, salt, or other medicinal compound to mix with water. You must monitor your dog's eyes after such a solution is administered; if the irritation persists, or if there is a significant discharge, immediate veterinary attention is warranted.

Your dog's *ears*, like his eyes, are extremely sensitive and can also be

Health and Disease

prone to infection, should wax and/or dirt be allowed to build up. Ear irritants may be present in the form of mites, soap or water, or foreign particles which the dog has come into contact with while romping through a wooded area. If your dog's ears are bothering him, you will know it—he will scratch his ears and shake his head, and the ears will have a foul-smelling dark secretion. This pasty secretion usually signals the onset of *otorrhea,* or ear canker, and at this stage proper veterinary care is essential if the dog's hearing is not to be permanently impaired. In the advanced stages of ear canker, tissue builds up within the ear, and the ear canal becomes blocked off, thus diminishing the hearing abilities of that ear. If this is to be prevented, you should wash your dog's ears, as they require it, with a very dilute solution of hydrogen peroxide and water, or an antibacterial ointment, as your vet suggests. In any case,

An ear mite.

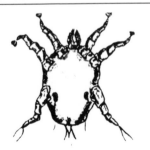

the ears, because of their delicacy, are to be washed gently, with a soft cloth or cotton.

Your pet's *teeth* can be maintained by his regular use of a chew product such as Nylabone® or Nylaball,® which serves to clean the teeth of tartar accumulation and to massage and stimulate the gums. Tartar accumulates on the teeth of dogs, particularly at the gum line, more rapidly than on the teeth of humans; and these accumulations, if not removed, bring irritation, infection and, ultimately, destruction of the teeth at the roots. With puppies, a chew product helps to relieve the discomfort of the teething stage and, of course, prevents the pup's chewing of your furniture and slippers! A periodic inspection of your dog's mouth will alert you to any problem he might have which would require a trip to the veterinarian's office. Any signs of tooth or gum sensitivity, redness, or swelling, signal the need for professional treatment.

A dog's *nails* should not be allowed to become overlong. If you live in a city and walk your dog regularly on pavement, chances are that his nails are kept trimmed from the "wear and tear" they receive from the sidewalks. However, if your dog gets all of his exercise in your yard, or if his nails simply

76

Health and Disease

grow rather quickly, it will occasionally be necessary for you to clip his nails. It is best for you to have your veterinarian show you the proper way to perform the nail clipping. Special care must always be taken to avoid cutting too far and reaching the "quick." If you cut into the quick of the nail, it will bleed, so it is easy to see why an expert must show you the proper procedure. A nail clipper designed especially for dogs can be purchased at any pet shop.

Emergency First Aid

If you fear that your dog has swallowed *poison,* immediately get him to the veterinarian's. Try to locate the source of poisoning; if he has swallowed, for example, a cleaning fluid kept in your house, check the bottle label to see if inducing the dog to vomit is necessary. Inducing the dog to vomit can be very harmful, depending upon the type of poison swallowed. Amateur diagnosis is very dangerous.

Accidents, unfortunately, do happen, so it is best to be prepared. If your dog gets hit by a car or has a bad fall, keep him absolutely quiet, move him as little as possible, and get veterinary treatment as soon as possible. It is unwise to give any stimulants such as brandy or other alcoholic liquids when there is visible external hemorrhage or the possibility of internal hemorrhaging.

Minor cuts and wounds will be licked by your dog, but you should treat such injuries as you would your own. Wash out the dirt and apply an antiseptic.

Severe cuts and wounds should be bandaged as tightly as possible to stop the bleeding. A wad of cotton may serve as a pressure bandage, which will ordinarily stop the flow of blood. Gauze wrapped around the cotton will hold it in place. Usually applying such pressure to a wound will sufficiently stop the blood flow; however, for severe bleeding, such as when an artery is cut, a tourniquet may be necessary. Apply a tourniquet between the injury and the heart if the bleeding is severe. To tighten the tourniquet, push a pencil through the bandage and twist it. Take your dog to a veterinarian immediately, since a tourniquet should not be left in place any longer than fifteen minutes.

Minor burns or scalds can be treated by clipping hair away from the affected area and then applying a paste of bicarbonate of soda and water. Apply it thickly to the burned area and try to keep the dog

Care of the Oldster

from licking it off.

Serious burns require the immediate attention of your veterinarian, as shock quickly follows such a burn. The dog should be kept quiet, wrapped in a blanket; and if he still shows signs of being chilled, use a hot-water bottle. Clean the burn gently, removing any foreign matter such as bits of lint, hair, grass, or dirt; and apply cold compresses. Act as quickly as possible. Prevent exposure to air by covering with gauze, cotton, and a loose bandage. To prevent the dog from interfering with the dressing, muzzle him and have someone stay with him until veterinary treatment is at hand.

Stings from wasps and bees are a hazard for the many dogs that enjoy trying to catch these insects. A sting frequently follows a successful catch, and it often occurs inside the mouth, which can be very serious. The best remedy is to get him to a veterinarian as soon as possible, but there are some precautionary measures to follow in the meantime. If the dog has been lucky enough to be stung only on the outside of the face, try to extricate the stinger; then swab the point of entry with a solution of bicarbonate of soda. In the case of a wasp sting, use vinegar or some other acidic food.

Barring accident or disease, your dog is apt to enjoy a life of 12 to 14 years. However, beginning roughly with the eighth year, there will be a gradual slowing down. And with this there are many problems of maintaining reasonably good health and comfort for all concerned.

While there is little or nothing that can be done in the instance of failing sight and hearing, proper management of the dog can minimize these losses. Fairly close and carefully supervised confinement are necessary in both cases. A blind dog, otherwise perfectly healthy and happy, can continue to be happy if he is always on a leash outdoors and guided so that he does not bump into things. Indoors, he will do well enough on his own. Dogs that are sightless seem to move around the house by their own radar system. They learn where objects are located; but once they do learn the pattern, care must be taken not to leave a piece of furniture out of its usual place.

Deafness again requires considerable confinement, especially in regard to motor traffic and similar hazards; but deafness curtails the dog's activities much less than blindness. It is not necessary to send any dog to the Great Beyond

Care of the Oldster

because it is blind or deaf—if it is otherwise healthy and seems to enjoy life.

Teeth in the aging dog should be watched carefully, not only for the pain they may cause the dog but also because they may poison the system without any local infection or pain. So watch carefully, especially when an old dog is eating. Any departure from his usual manner should make the teeth suspect at once. Have your veterinarian check the teeth frequently.

His System Slows Down

As the dog ages and slows down in his physical activity, so his whole system slows down. With the change, physical functions are in some instances slowed and in others accelerated—in effect, at least.

For example, constipation may occur; and bowel movements may become difficult, infrequent, or even painful. Chronic constipation is a problem for your veterinarian to deal with; but unless it is chronic, it is easily dealt with by adding a little extra melted fat to the regular food. Do not increase roughage or administer physics unless so directed by your veterinarian. If the added

fat in the food doesn't seem to be the answer to occasional constipation, give your dog a half or a full teaspoon of mineral oil two or three times a week. Otherwise, call your veterinarian.

On either side of the rectal opening just below the base of the tail are located the two anal glands. Occasionally these glands do not function properly and may cause the dog great discomfort if not cleaned out. This is a job for your veterinarian, until after he has shown you how to do it.

Watch His Weight

In feeding the aging dog, try to keep his weight down. He may want just as much to eat as ever, but with

An easy way to weigh your dog is to hold the dog while you stand on a scale, and then subtract your weight from the total.

Care of the Oldster

decreased activity he will tend to put on weight. This weight will tend to slow down all other bodily functions and place an added strain on the heart. So feed the same diet as usual, but watch the weight.

Age, with its relaxing of the muscles, frequently makes an otherwise clean dog begin to misbehave in the house, particularly so far as urination is concerned. There is little that can be done about it, if your veterinarian finds there is no infection present, except to give your dog more frequent chances to urinate and move his bowels. It's just a little bit more work on your part to keep your old friend more comfortable and a "good" dog.

Let your dog exercise as much as he wants to without encouraging him in any violent play. If he is especially sluggish, take him for a walk on a leash in the early morning or late evening. Avoid exercise for him during the heat of the day. And in cold weather or rain, try a sweater on him when he goes out. It's not "sissy" to put a coat on an old dog. You and your veterinarian, working closely together, can give your dog added life and comfort. So consult your veterinarian often.

Occasionally in an old dog there is a problem of unpleasant smell, both bodily and orally. If this situation is acute, it is all but unbearable to have the dog around. But the situation can be corrected or at least alleviated with frequent and rather heavy dosing of chlorophyll. A good rubdown with one of the dry-shampoo products is also helpful.

When the End Comes

People who have dogs are sooner or later faced with the tragedy of losing them. It's tough business losing a dog, no matter how many you may have at one time. And one dog never takes the place of another—so don't expect it to. When you lose your dog, get another as quickly as you can. It does help a lot.

Keep your dog alive as long as he is happy and comfortable. Do everything you reasonably can to keep him that way. But when the sad time comes that he is sick, always uncomfortable, or in some pain, it is your obligation then to have him put away. It is a tough ordeal to go through, but you owe it to your old friend to allow him to go to sleep. And, literally, that's just what he does. Your veterinarian knows what to do. And your good old dog, without pain, fright, bad taste, or bad smells, will just drift to sleep.